# CHICAGO

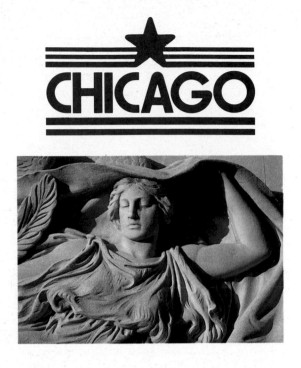

This book was devised and produced by
Multimedia Publications (UK) Ltd

**Editor: Marilyn Inglis**
**Design: John Strange and Associates**
**Picture Research: Tessa Paul**
**Production: Arnon Orbach**

ISBN 0 8317 1253 8

First published in the United States of
America 1985 by Gallery Books, an imprint of
W. H. Smith Publishers Inc., 112 Madison
Avenue, New York, NY 10016

Typeset by Flowery Typesetters Ltd
Originated by Imago Publishing Ltd
Printed by Sagdos, Milan, Italy

# CHICAGO

Carole Chester

**GALLERY BOOKS**
An Imprint of W. H. Smith Publishers Inc.
112 Madison Avenue
New York City 10016

# Contents

# America's Second City

It has given its name to a musical and to one of Frank Sinatra's hit songs. It has been home to gangsters and speakeasies. It is notorious for being "The Windy City" and also has a great name for jazz. Was Chicago ever a "toddlin' town"? Perhaps so, at its roots, but today it is the hub of the Midwest; gateway to the Great Lakes; a major trade and transportation center—America's "Second City".

Chicago has the size to match its temperature range (and that's from below freezing in winter to high humidity in summer), but it also has style. Considered one of the world's most modern cities architecturally, it boasts the world's tallest skyscraper. And in addition to that, the city's School of Architecture produced those geniuses, Louis Henri Sullivan and Frank Lloyd Wright. There is an elegance about many of its buildings and boulevards. It is a city of arts and parks.

Boring Chicago can't be, though brash it sometimes is. Peaceful it might have been in the days when the Potawatomi tribe lived in the area in the 1600s, but later times gave the "Second City" flamboyance, exuberance. It was—and is—spirited, aided and abetted by vast swarms of subsequent immigrants who also settled at the lakeside and helped turn it into an ethnic melting pot.

Always a trading post, Chicago benefited from its immigrants, who added their own knowledge, expertise and talents. Trade and industry took on new meanings that even the Great Fire of 1871 couldn't burn out. The "foreigners" brought their craft skills with them and their musical abilities.

Chicago has known aggression, violence, and vice of all kinds, yet the very aggression which has given it a bad name is also responsible for its growth and strength. (It ranks first in the US production of iron and steel, electrical equipment, supplies and machinery, as well as in the construction industry.) Its curiosity has provided it with famous newspapers, writers, critics and musicians. And its naturally beautiful setting has softened its commerciality.

This vintage sailing vessel on Lake Michigan lends an old world atmosphere to its modern high rise backdrop – the city's "Loop" downtown area.

Business-minded Chicago equally has its pleasures. It is ostentatious but also subtle. It gets funky but also has its tranquil moments. Big City appeal – superb shops, fine restaurants, vibrant nightlife – is Chicago's lure for the tourist. Big-time contracts and cold hard cash turns on corporations. Don't expect Chicago to be sleepy – it's one grown-up city, with grown-up interests on its mind.

Taking on Chicago is taking on raw adventure. However, "class" is not far away. Love it or hate it, the city has a magnificence all can feel. A little infamy never hurt anyone; a little finesse adds culture. Chicago smugly claims both. Bright lights . . . guts . . . positivity . . . charm . . . you name it!

The city is large enough to boast 75 distinct neighborhoods, and from the visitor's point of view, it can be split into zones: Downtown; The Loop; The Magnificent Mile; North Side; South Side; Lincoln Park. Skytop views, lakeside views; jam-packed views and green green views. All within its grasp. Did you know a third of America's population lives within 500 miles of this major metropolis – one reason why Chicago is the Midwest Giant?

*Above left* Business carries on even when the weather is icy. Chicagoans are used to it. After all, they survived a great 1979 blizzard, proving yet again how hardy and spirited they really are.

*Below left* They don't call it "The Windy City" for nothing and in winter there's snow to contend with as well. Most recommended times for visiting are spring and fall when the weather is at its most kind.

*Below* Winter in the Midwest means the car may have to stay where it is; the house looks pristine white and the telephone lines get frozen with icicles. Anyone seen the skis?

*Right* Michigan Avenue is one of the city's busiest thoroughfares so the cops are often out directing traffic. Part of the avenue is named "The Magnificent Mile" for its glamorous shops.

*Below* Summertime is festival time in Chicago. One of the special July events is the sailboat race on Lake Michigan and, pictured here, a sailing regatta takes place on the river.

*Left* The public transportation system is good but it's easy enough to hail a taxi. Chicago has four recognized companies: American United, Checker, Flash and the Yellow Cab Company.

*Below* This colorful mural is typical of what you might find in Old Town where high class stores are next to honky tonks and cloistered restaurants next to folk bars. The main street is Wells.

*Far left* Chicago gave birth to the skyscraper so it's only right it claims two of the world's tallest buildings. The invention of the elevator and Jenney's use of steel frame construction made all this possible.

*Above left* Cycling's one way to keep fit and enjoy the scenery of the lakefront and Lincoln Park. Visitors may rent bikes from park concessions in the summer months.

*Below left* First National Plaza's a great place for a brown bag lunch. Office workers come here for a quick sunbathe but also stop to enjoy Chagall's "Four Seasons" mural decorating the outside lower level.

# Architectural Wonders

Though it was a terrible city fire which killed over 300 people and left thousands homeless, destroying Chicago's downtown, one result was the birth of the skyscraper. Much of the city was redesigned by some of America's most talented architects, and in 1884 William Le Baron Jenney built that first soaring structure. After that, there was no looking back. Frank Lloyd Wright became the pioneer of the low-slung, prairie-style house. Architect Daniel Burnham laid out the plan for the multitude of city parks in 1909. While other cities pulled down buildings, Chicago's rose, surrounded with pedestrian plazas decorated with modern sculpture masterpieces by Chagall, Picasso, Calder and others.

One of the few structures to survive the 1871 fire was the Old Water Tower, completed in 1869. Located on Michigan Avenue, Chicago's historic pumping station has continued to supply millions of gallons of water to the people of Chicago. Nowadays, this famous city landmark is open to visitors who can see and learn about Chicago's water system on a narrated tour. In addition, a multi-screen film-show about the city is presented in the Tower's special theater.

The oldest skyscraper, steel-framed, is the Manhattan Building, dating from 1891, and located at 431 South Dearborn. It was this construction method, pioneered by Le Baron Jenney, which enabled architects of a later era to build skyscrapers as we know them today.

Built in 1886, the Rookery is the world's oldest remaining steel-skeleton skyscraper. Situated on South LaSalle Street, it was designed by Holabird and Root. Its famous stairwell and handsome lobby were remodeled by Frank Lloyd Wright in 1905. The Monadnock Building at 53 West Jackson is still the highest commercial building which has outside walls of masonry construction, while the Marquette Building at 140 South Dearborn (constructed by Holabird and Root in 1894) influenced the design of many other subsequent multi-story office buildings.

The Rookery, originally a temporary city hall, was so named because it seemed to be a favorite rendezvous for pigeons.

One of Chicago's most impressive landmarks, particularly at night when it is illuminated, is the Wrigley Building on North Michigan Avenue. You can't miss this white monolith, built in two sections and designed in French Renaissance style. Nor the one across the street – the Tribune Tower, a neo-Gothic skyscraper that is home to the *Chicago Tribune*.

Banking is no game in this town – there are 81 commercial and 23 savings banks. What is claimed to be the world's tallest bank building is the First National Bank of Chicago on Dearborn and Madison Streets whose plaza contains a 70 foot long mosaic designed by Marc Chagall and entitled "The Four Seasons".

Unusual sculptures set off a number of the city buildings' plazas. At the Civic Center, seat of city and county governments on Randolph and Clark Streets, stands the 50 ft high Pablo Picasso sculpture. Picasso liked the city so much that he designed this artwork especially for Chicago, though he gave it no name. Another piece, "Flamingo", caused some controversy when it was placed in front of the Federal Center at Adams and Dearborn Streets. Designed by Alexander Calder, this sculpture stands 52 ft high.

Harry Bertoia's "Sounding Sculpture" is set in a reflecting pool in front of the Standard Oil Building on East Randolph Street. The building is the world's fourth tallest building at a height of 1136 feet. Until New York goes one better, Chicago has the prize for height with its glossy Sears Tower on Wacker Drive and Jackson – 110 stories and 1454 ft tall. It's the best place for a panoramic view of the city: it can be seen in all its splendor from the 103rd floor Skydeck (1365 ft up). Speaking of observation decks, "Big John" has one too. Though the John Hancock Center on North Michigan lost one title to the Sears Tower, it is still the world's tallest residential office building, with an observation tower open daily and worth visiting. Before climbing skyward at the Sears Tower, by the way, stop a moment in the lobby to look at "Universe", a motorized mural by Alexander Calder.

*Above left* The suburb of Oak Park is where Frank Lloyd Wright lived during his early Chicago years and began his career. Some 25 of his buildings remain in the area including this outstanding example of his work.

*Below Left* The foremost Frank Lloyd Wright building in Chicago is Robie House, built in 1909 at 5757 South Woodlawn. Note his 'prairie style' architectural design which, despite the date, gives this house a particularly contemporary look.

*Above* This stained glass detail shows Wright's incredible feel for design. He was greatly influenced by Louis Sullivan whose firm he worked for when he first arrived from Wisconsin. His own career spanned more than 70 years!

*Below* Few buildings have greater architectural flair and distinction than The Rookery. A masonry construction, this building embodied many innovative technical features which were to become widely used.

Other buildings worth noting include the Chicago Public Library; Lake Point Tower and Harbor Point Tower (both apartment blocks on the waterfront, interesting for their shape); Marina City, Dearborn Street at the Chicago River (twin cylindrically-shaped 60-story apartment buildings); and the Auditorium Theater, designed by Louis Sullivan.

Because of its pride in its architecture, Chicago offers visitors guided tours and it's worth noting that the Glessner House on South Prairie, a renovated nineteenth-century mansion designed by Henry Hobson Richardson, is headquarters of the Chicago School of Architecture.

Visitors are welcome to admire the Elks National Monument and Headquarters, dedicated to Elks who served in both world wars. The handsomely designed building features a rotunda and reception rooms ornamented with marble, murals, sculpture and beautiful wood paneling.

Another interesting building is that of the University of Illinois, whose campus is superbly laid out. Hull House on the Chicago Circle Campus was established by Jane Addams, not only a pioneer social worker but the first American woman to win the Nobel Peace Prize.

Style even spreads itself to the city's shops and hotels. Carson Pirie Scott, *the* Chicago place to shop, at State and Madison Streets, was Louis Sullivan's last major building and is considered by many to be his masterpiece. The gracious Drake Hotel (now a Hilton) was constructed as a luxury hotel in the early 1900s on an area that was previously water (Lake Michigan). It is now listed in the National Register of Historic Places.

It is only appropriate perhaps that the site of the Great Fire is today the Chicago Fire Academy building. At the time of the fire there was a property on the site belonging to the O'Learys, and story has it that it

*Above right* The Manhattan Building on "The Loop" was designed by William Le Baron Jenney and built in 1890 and is the city's oldest standing steel-framed building. Jenney pioneered this construction method which made today's skyscrapers possible.

*Below right* The Union Carbide Building on North Michigan Avenue is another example of why Chicago is famed for its fine and varied architecture.

*Left* Pictured are the Chicago River bridges in the North Loop area. In the background is the landmark Wrigley Building which gave upper Michigan Avenue its sophistication in 1924. Still admired for its somewhat eccentric lines, the Wrigley remains a Chicago favorite.

started when Mrs O'Leary's cow kicked over a lighted lantern in the barn. Well, maybe so and maybe not. It certainly began on this very spot but the exact cause will probably never be known. To symbolize the event, though, a bronze sculpture, not surprisingly entitled "Tongues of Flame", by Egon Weiner, is located on a paved plaza outside the Academy.

Water is the only thing for fires which is perhaps why Chicagoans are said to have the largest fountain in the world – Buckingham Fountain on the lakefront, at Grant Park. Between May and September when the fountain is turned on, there is a nightly colorful light show here. For the statisticians, the fountain holds about 1.5 million gallons of water and the main spout shoots water 145 feet into the air.

*Above* The fantastic Marina Towers apartment building at Dearborn and the river was the architectural center of attention for years. Inaugurated in 1964, it was the first of a spate of office/apartment blocks which offered living, working and recreational facilities under one roof.

*Right* The 333 North Wacker Drive building, jointly designed by New York and Chicago architects, has become a popular attraction with tourists who come to admire the reflective quality of its windows.

*Facing page, left* View from the waterfront of the North Michigan Avenue skyline. Beside the Water Tower Building stands "Big John", the world's second tallest building – the John Hancock Center. Its fame for being the tallest building was short-lived but its observation deck still offers a magnificent city view.

*Below* Lake Point Tower Apartments up-staged Marina Towers by being even more of an architectural masterpiece. This undulating glass tower follows a design by Mies van der Rohe and Skidmore's John Hancock Center. It is also an office/apartment combination about ten feet shorter than the Empire State.

*Right* An unusual viewpoint of the skyline seen from Buckingham fountain where bronze monsters play. Chicago is a city of fountains – one can be found in virtually every patch of green.

*Far right* Photographed against Wacker Drive stands Union Station. It was the rail network for distributing corn and wheat that formed the basis of the city's economy in the latter half of the nineteenth century. In 1856, Chicago had become the nation's largest rail center and it continues to be the hub of the Midwest.

*Below* The newest of Nieman-Marcus branches in Chicago is this one on North Michigan Avenue, opened at the end of 1983. The name is synonymous with fine merchandise for this Texas-headquartered department store where the best of the best is for sale. Noted for its chic merchandise, brand names include greats like Nina Ricci, Hermès, Ungaro, Charles Jourdan and Valentino.

*Right* The old Water Tower is a landmark, a survivor of Chicago's great 1871 fire. It now serves as a visitor information center where multimedia presentations are given and the city's unique water system is explained on a guided tour.

*Above* Best known building designed by Louis Sullivan is Carson Pirie Scott department store which is particularly ornamented above its State and Madison Street entrance. The architect considered this to be his masterpiece and, in accordance with its significance as a landmark, it contains some of the best merchandise found anywhere in the city.

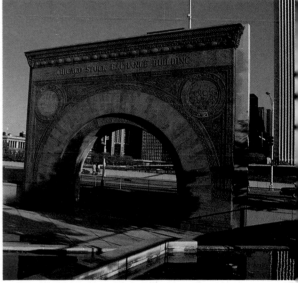

*Above* Louis Sullivan's magnificent Stock Exchange Arch and reflecting pool. Unfortunately, the Sullivan Stock Exchange itself was torn down some years ago. (Sullivan was famous for rich and highly original ornamentation and several of his buildings still survive in the city.)

*Left* It's a long way up there when it comes to cleaning windows and in Chicago one needs a good head for heights. The building which can't be missed in this photograph is the landmark Wrigley, famous for its ostentation.

# People

Survivors! Chicagoans have always been that. Be it riots, blizzards, or massacres, survivors have triumphed. After all, this site was a mere wild onion patch – hence the Indian name – *Chi-ca-gow* meaning onion patch. Then came the white men – Louis Jolliet and Jacques Marquette, stopping en route to Canada in 1673.

Chicago today has a large black population, so perhaps it is only appropriate that the first proper settler was in fact not white, but a Negro fur trader by the name of Jean Baptiste du Sable, who established a trading post on the north bank of the mouth of the Chicago River. His cabin is thought to have been located close to where the Tribune Tower is today.

His may have been the first permanent settlement, but it didn't take long for Chicago to grow. In 1833 it was a village with 350 residents. By 1871, the population had increased to over 330 000, by which time it was known as a city. Many of those people came from Poland, Germany and other European countries. By 1850, it was the Irish who formed the majority of Chicago's foreign-born population whereas today there are more Poles here than in any other city outside of Warsaw. Old Town is a restored German settlement dating from the 1870s whose architecture remains typically Germanic with a number of buildings that have stained glass windows.

Waves of immigrants came to this area of America to work in its growing industries and till the land. Not only the Germans and Poles, but Scandinavians, Italians, Greeks and Yugoslavs besides. Some worked on the railway; some farmed; some worked in the grain and manufacturing industries. By 1890, some 80 per cent of the city's population were immigrants, or descended from immigrants. And some became millionaires whose names linger on.

Looks like the fleet's in and there's no better place to enjoy some summer sunshine than Lincoln Park. Named for President Lincoln, the park is very popular with Chicagoans and also visitors – it houses a zoo and a conservatory where there are displays of plants and flowers from around the world, year round. It's the city's largest park and is surrounded by one of the most affluent neighborhoods.

The ethnic heritage has given today's Chicago its flavor, its color, its neighborhoods. For the best of cuisine, try the lakeview neighborhood to about 3400 North where there is diversity to beat all – Mexican, Chinese, German. Southwest of Michigan Avenue and Adams you'll find Greektown where some of the city's best, and cheapest, restaurants are located.

Further south, near 22nd and Wentworth Avenue, is Chicago's own Chinatown and, on Taylor Street, Little Italy, where you can find home-made ice cream, pasta like mama makes and all the etceteras. It all goes to show that Chicago is made up of more than prime rib steaks, even though it was here that meat packers made their name. The Swifts, Armours, Libby and Wilson were eventually to become internationally known for their meats.

For sure, Chicago has had its favorite – and unfavorite – sons. Those who found fortune; those who were flamboyant. There was Mrs Potter Palmer, the hostess, who lived in an opulent mansion and served nothing but the best. There was eccentric Captain George Streeter who tried to form his own separate state named "Streeterville", which he said "wouldn't have a Chamber of Commerce until it had a cabaret".

*Far left* A green Chicago River because it's St Patrick's Day! The city has always boasted a large Irish population – in 1850 the Irish formed the largest group of foreign-born residents. Today, Bridgeport is a predominantly Irish neighborhood.

*Above left* Chicago is a notable seat of learning with several fine universities whose libraries are crammed with knowledge. It has spawned many famous writers including Saul Bellow and Richard Stern. Every important poet has had work published here and the city is home to one of America's oldest newspapers.

*Below left* With a true love for Irish revelry, St Patrick's Day Parade brings out the most colorful costumes and devil-may-care antics. Chicago comprises a number of ethnic quarters, each with its own festivals, but St Paddy's Day remains one of the liveliest.

The architects won acclaim; the gangsters, notoriety. Prohibition brought Chicago riches but also its sinful reputation. Gang warfare may not be what Chicago wishes to remember most, but gangster heroes like Al Capone have placed this city on every person's private map. Yes, there was a mob-style massacre here on St Valentine's Day in 1929 – an event which has been the subject of books and movies. An event long gone, but, yes, it is famous of its kind. Reform didn't come easily for those who relished the gaudy frolics. As the last of the old saloon-keeping aldermen, Paddy Bauler, continued to say: "Chicago ain't ready for reform yet."

No matter – the gambling saloons and brothels that used to be associated with the city are no more, but that doesn't mean to say nightlife isn't plentiful. It is. One of the most excitingly busy and neon-lit streets is Rush Street – an entertainment district that stretches between Chestnut and Division Streets. Jazz spots, movie theaters, discotheques. Music that ranges from soul and blues to hard rock, to folk. There is even belly dancing.

There's action, too, in Old Town from around 1200 to 1700 North on Wells Street where an evening's amusement doesn't require straying far. A cobblestoned alleyway … gas lamps … clubs in Victorian style. And in New Town, where the young professionals live, from 2400 to 3400 North on Clark Street and 2200 to 2800 North Lincoln Avenue. Though Chicago may have been at its most prosperous and frenetic in the Twenties when it was home to many US artists, including Carl Sandburg and Benny Goodman, it is just as vivacious today and a lot less violent.

If the city loves razzmatazz, it equally loves sports. Indeed, a sportier town would be hard to find. There's a fervor about Chicagoans, and character, both amongst the sportsmen and their fans. The Bears are the pro football team, and when in town they play at Soldier Field. This stadium by the waterfront is the NFL's oldest and a fine one for football viewers. The Black Hawks used to be a powerhouse national hockey team, and The Bulls are Chicago's pro basketball team. Both teams play at the Chicago stadium just west of downtown.

*Top right* Chicago is a city of multinationals with restaurants for every conceivable type of cuisine. Here on the south side Poles and Bohemians predominate.

*Middle right* Greektown has plenty of good inexpensive restaurants and family-owned grocery shops, all within a few blocks of each other around 300 South Halstead. A pleasant area for an evening out.

*Facing page, bottom* A stein of beer is readily available in any of Chicago's many German restaurants. Germans were among the numerous immigrants who headed this way in the late eighteenth century and Old Town itself is a restored German settlement with typical architecture.

*Left* There are more Poles in Chicago than anywhere else outside of Warsaw although in 1850 they made up less than one per cent of the city. There are several predominantly Polish districts including this delightful small community around the Milwaukee area where food shopping is an adventurous experience.

*Below* Over the years waves of immigrants have brought their traditions and way of life to Chicago. Not only their food and their folklore but religion as well. This church is one used by the Armenian community.

*Right* A good number of Chicago's large black population live on the south side. As it so happens the first real settler, Jean Baptiste du Sable, was also black. A fur trader, he came here in the 1770s and built a log cabin on the north river bank.

*Below* That's entertainment – and Chicago has plenty of it, from street singers to soul, rock and jazz. Visitors can enjoy watching the little-knowns and the well-knowns in plush nightclubs, dimly-lit bars and in summer in the parks.

Soccer is played almost year-round, outdoors in spring and summer and indoors the rest of the year. Chicago's own team is The Sting. Wrigley Field, north of downtown, is the site for Chicago Cub games and Comiskey Park is the home of the White Sox. The oldest park in baseball, Comiskey was built by Charles Comiskey and the first game was played in 1910.

Chicagoans are shoppers and the shops are superb. That's how the Magnificent Mile got its name. Along this section of North Michigan Avenue, from the Chicago River to Oak Street, there are dazzling windows to tempt browsers and buyers alike. Some of the stores here are famous names: Marshall Field, Lord & Taylor, Saks, and Gucci. But there are glamorous boutiques as well. Water Tower Place is the best point to start at – a seven-level atrium shopping mall that houses major department stores and specialty shops, restaurants and theaters.

That "great street", State Street, is another prime shopping area running parallel to Wabash Avenue. Between Congress and Wacker Drive is a pedestrian mall where you'll find fashionable stores and sidewalk cafés. Rococo Carson Pirie Scott is here on State Street and so is Lyttons. Popcorn vendors and roasted chestnut stands offer tasty tidbits while street entertainers supply an aura of merrymaking.

For unusual shopping, head for Oak Street, to the friendly block that runs from Michigan Avenue to Rush Street, where there's not much that is commonplace. Or to Old Town, where the shops are small and interesting. The elegant and chic might shop too in the Lincoln Park West area and in Chicago's handsome suburban malls.

Find the ethnic neighborhoods – almost every nationality has its own shops, museum and certainly its customs. In Chicago there are Swedes, Chinese, Ukrainians, Sicilians, Greeks, Irish, Italians, Lithuanians, Poles, Latins and blacks.

All of them love the city's plazas where programs of special events take place, where a brown bag lunch is as much fun as an *à la carte* restaurant – together they give Chicago its rhythm and electricity.

State Street is a prime shopping street with a pedestrian mall lined with fashionable stores and sidewalk cafés. Street vendors are here, too, offering fresh flowers and tasty tidbits whilst street entertainers add a party atmosphere.

33

*Left above* Chinatown at 22nd and Wentworth is marked by pagoda-shaped roofs on buildings and telephone boxes. The neighborhood is filled with first class restaurants, interesting grocery stores and curio shops. The biggest celebration takes place here at Chinese New Year.

*Left below* Two Vietnamese boys share a joke. Chicago's Oriental population isn't limited to the Chinese whose ranks have been swollen by immigrants from other Far Eastern countries. For over a hundred years, the city has been a melting pot for many different nationalities.

*Far left* A celebration day for the Poles brings out the children in national dress. The Polish are as fond of festivities as they are of good food and drink and comprise one of the largest segments of Chicago's population. Many live around the Milwaukee area.

*Right* A Christmas card winter scene in Chicago as a horse-drawn carriage waits patiently for customers. In the background, the old Water Tower remains one of the few survivors of the Great Fire during which much of the downtown was destroyed.

*Far right, above* Many parades take place in Chicago throughout the year, often stemming from differing ethnic origins. This one, however, is to celebrate Christmas and is for everyone.

*Far right, below* The Heritage Parade down Michigan Avenue was designed to show the city's mixed ethnic background. In addition to the Poles, Germans and Irish, there are Mexicans, Greeks, Swedes and many others adding local color to this parade.

# Making Money

America's busiest airport... the world's largest grain exchange... a major trade and transportation center... home to many Fortune 500 companies. That's Chicago. Number one convention city, a communications hub for the Midwest and a financial center second only to New York, where billions of dollars turn over in both wholesale and retail business.

Chicago became the world's busiest rail center between 1848 and 1856, and it is still the heart of Amtrak's network. O'Hare International Airport on the city's outskirts is served by numerous international and domestic airlines, and claims to be the world's busiest, with yearly passenger traffic estimated at over 38 million. Lake Michigan, too, plays its part, being the port of entry for steamships and freighters coming from Europe via the St Lawrence Seaway. (Chicago's ports handle well over 82 million tons of freight each year.)

Transportation is important because of industry and while Chicagoans have been careful not to spoil their lakefront, industry abounds. The city ranks number one in America for the production of steel, commercial printing, furniture marketing, radio and TV manufacturing, mail order, industrial machinery manufacturing, confectionery and musical instruments. Nuclear research and the electronics industry came of age in Chicago. Half the radar equipment used during World War Two was made here.

In the 1980s, Chicago does something like $90 billion annually in wholesale trade and $332 billion in retail. Some of that retail trade is done in the city's famed department store, Marshall Field & Company. When it was built in 1892 it was quite something. Electric light was not common in those days and the store was designed in sections with shopping areas on balconies overlooking a skylit central courtyard. Later, the skylights were covered over, one by a blue and gold Louis Tiffany mosaic which you can still see if you enter at the first Randolph Street door east of State. Besides

Construction never ceases. There's always a taller building on the rise. Work here is going on at Number 1 Park Place on Michigan Avenue, illustrating that the Chicago area ranks first in the construction industry.

the more mundane, Marshall Field sells luxury goods like copper-roofed dolls' houses worth thousands of dollars.

As for manufacturing, there are around 14 000 plants in the greater metropolitan area employing a million people. Around 90 per cent of America's grain deliveries are contracted at the Chicago Board of Trade, the world's largest grain exchange. Visitors may watch the gesticulating and the trading from an upper gallery, keeping an eye on the electronic record of all the trades displayed. The Board's operations are explained in a film and slide presentation and it's all for free. The action is similar at the Chicago Mercantile Exchange and International Money Market on West Jackson, the world's largest commodity futures exchange trading market. Visitors are welcome on weekdays and actually sit down to watch.

Another world's largest is the Merchandise Mart on Wells Street at the Chicago River, a commercial buying center that covers two city blocks. Where is all the money kept? In a bounty of banks. They're not all as stylish as the First National, but there are plenty of them – well over a hundred have headquarters in the city.

Money – $35 million to be precise – donated by John D. Rockefeller in the early 1900s helped to make the private University of Chicago among the top ten research institutions in America and the birthplace of nuclear energy. Money – lots of it – comes in with the conventioneers. Chicago has been a favorite venue for conferences and exhibitions for years. Way back in 1893 the city hosted the World's Columbian Exposition which attracted 27 million visitors, about 50 per cent of America's total population at that time. The 1933 Century of

*Facing page, above* Arrivees by train get off at Union Station. Chicago is an important stop for Amtrak's rail system and rail connections have helped the city become the major manufacturing and commercial center it is today. Between 1848 and 1856, it was the world's busiest rail center.

*Facing page, below* O'Hare International Airport is America's busiest bringing thousands of visitors daily to the Midwest. Every minute sees flight departures and arrivals. So vast is the area that O'Hare has become a 'Second City' with hotel, restaurant and entertainment facilities all concentrated around the airport itself.

*Left* A sophisticated public transportation system makes it easy to get around the city. "The Loop", lake front and suburbs can all be reached by several methods including the "El" train whose platform and passengers are pictured here.

*Below* The elevated train known simply and affectionately as "The El" encircles "The Loop" which generally speaking is the city's business district. Indeed, it was the looping section of elevated train tracks that gave downtown its nickname.

*Right* About 90 per cent of America's grain deliveries are contracted at the Chicago Board of Trade on West Jackson Boulevard. Inside, it's a colorful affair with runners in bright jackets delivering orders and an electronic record of all trades displayed overhead.

Progress Exposition was another gargantuan celebration. That 1893 exercize, by the way, was the reason Chicago got its "Windy City" title – or so it is said. A New York newspaper coined it when New York was vying with Chicago for the exposition. It was not, however, referring to the elements (average lakefront winds are about ten mph), but to the windiness of the Chicago politicians! Chicago got the World's Fair but it also got stuck with its nickname.

The Wall Street of the Midwest is LaSalle, where all the major banks are located. Some of the people who bank here live in the ritzy apartments lining Lake Shore Drive. Others – the YUPPIES (young urban professionals) live in the Lincoln Park and New Town areas. Indeed, Lincoln Park is one of Chicago's most affluent neighborhoods. And where are the rich buried? Some of the city's former hotel barons and steel magnates are buried in Graceland Cemetery on the city's North side. Here, too, are the tombs of architects Louis Sullivan and Daniel Burnham.

There have been, and still are, many famous moneyed names in Chicago. One of the effects of the Civil War was a hugely increased demand for grain, which meant that the time was ripe for anyone in the farm implement business. Cyrus H. McCormick happened to be in the right place at the right time. He began manufacturing his McCormick reaper in 1848 at the start of the grain boom and had a factory in full swing by the start of the Civil War, just when it was needed.

The first steel rail in the USA was rolled in Chicago in 1865 and George M. Pullman's Palace Car Company was established about the same time. He founded the nation's first company town in 1880 – Pullman Community on the South side, which is now a national landmark.

In the 1860s, Potter Palmer and Marshall Field established their dry goods store and we know what a success that was. After the Great Fire, Philip D. Armour and Gustavus F. Swift founded their famous meat packing businesses and within a few years turned Chicago into the world's meat packing capital.

*Left* The Chicago Board of Trade is the world's largest and oldest commodity futures trading market. Trading seen here on the agricultural floor may be viewed from the visitors' gallery on the fifth floor while a multimedia presentation explains all the Board's activities.

*Below* All the gesticulations of trading may be viewed at the Chicago Mercantile Exchange, the world's largest futures market in perishable goods. Futures are traded in livestock, agricultural commodities, forest products etc.

After World War One, Chicagoans' new money tempted others to try to relieve them of it, and prohibition gave the impetus for a new industry — bootlegging. Profits were enormous and so criminal gangs became more and more ruthless. Jim Colosimo, head of one, became known as "the father of organized crime" while Al Capone hit the jackpot at the early age of twenty-five with 700 people working for him.

Thanks to money Chicago has its Buckingham Fountain, donated by spinster heiress Kate Buckingham who inherited the fortune made by her father from grain, banking, insurance and elevated railroads. She had the money to indulge her whims but was also socially generous. Not only did she spend $750 000 to build the fountain and a further $300 000 for its upkeep, but she left $2 000 000 to the Arts Institute and $1 000 000 for a nine-foot monument to Alexander Hamilton.

There is still a Palmer House in Chicago, though it's not the original hotel built by Potter Palmer — that went in the fire. Nor does the present day Palmer House boast a barber shop floor inlaid with silver dollars, as the pre-fire hostelry was said to have done, but it is a city legend still.

*Far left* Chicago claims it is first in the U.S. in the construction industry as well as in the production of iron and steel, electrical equipment and machinery supplies. Prior to the Great Fire, most buildings had been built of wood.

*Left* As a result of a 1794 Indian battle, land at the mouth of the Chicago River was acquired by the U.S. and a prosperous lake port quickly grew. But it was the opening of the Saint Lawrence Seaway which changed it from lakeport to seaport — at the crossroads of the U.S.

*Below* The imposing building overlooking a sailboat regatta taking place on the Chicago River is the Merchandise Mart, the world's largest trade center. It is reckoned that Chicago does around $90 billion in wholesale trade. Tours of the Mart are available.

*Far left* Prime shoppers' delight is Water Tower Place, a gleaming 74-story high-rise combination of stores, restaurants, theaters, offices and apartments. Famous Marshall Field's is just one of many stores reached by the Michigan Avenue entrance into the covered atrium mall.

*Left* Of the 600 or so periodicals and newspapers published in Chicago, the *Tribune,* established in 1847, is the city's oldest English-language paper. It was helped to maturity by Medill, Patterson and McCormick and occupies the Tribune Tower building.

*Below* The city is a major center for food production. Seen here is one of Chicago's main bakeries.

# Cultural Wealth

It was while the gangsters were fighting it out that Chicago began to develop its cultural side. The Art Institute, for example, grew to a museum of international importance during the 1920s and 1930s. Today it houses a superb collection of paintings dating from the fourteenth century and including a particularly fine set from the French Impressionists. Monet and Manet are well represented and in fact were exhibited here as long ago as 1895 when other world museums were not so sure of their importance. The museum also houses beautiful Oriental works, drawings and prints.

Originally the Art Institute began as an academy where people could study art as well as view it back in the 1880s. By comparison, the Museum of Contemporary Art is very new. It is also small but always lively with many changing exhibitions of work by contemporary artists.

Much of Chicago's cultural life began in the 1800s. The city's Symphony Orchestra – America's third oldest – made its debut in 1891, but it wasn't until 1971, 80 years later, that it had its first international tour. Visitors can enjoy performances in its own hall (designed by Daniel Burnham) across Michigan Avenue from the Art Institute. In summer, the Orchestra plays a series of open-air concerts during the Ravinia Festival in a park 25 miles north of The Loop. Bus and train service is available to Ravinia, where music lovers can choose full dining facilities or a sit-on-the-grass picnic.

The Lyric Opera Company came into being in 1858 though it wasn't really until 1954, when backers brought Maria Callas to the US stage for the first time, that it had any sparkle. The opera season runs from September through December and the repertoire is an adventurous one.

Millionaires of the day did more than just make money for themselves. They also gave the city culture and finesse.

The Art Institute of Chicago houses an excellent collection of Impressionist and post-Impressionist paintings among other items. Founded as an art school in 1893, it grew to importance as a museum during the 1920s and 1930s.

Sometimes it took a little coercing, as it did with Marshall Field, who initially refused to part with money to help preserve the vast collection of natural history specimens remaining after the 1893 Exposition, but who was eventually persuaded to give first one million, then eight more. Thanks mostly to his money, Chicago got its Field Museum. The building, designed by Burnham, is impressive, with its Georgia marble exterior, 706 feet long. And its contents are fascinating.

Chicago is a city of museums, from the well-known to specialist ones highlighting Polish history, health or Chicago's own past. Another of the best-known is the Museum of Science and Industry, full of buttons to push, wheels to turn and things to explore – such as a full-sized coal mine and a captured German U-boat. Scientific principles are shown in 75 exhibit halls where, among other things, visitors can trace the evolution of automobile, rail and airline transportation.

At the John G. Shedd Aquarium, the Coral Reef Exhibit is the most popular when a diver enters to hand-feed the three hundred plus colorful fish living in this 90 000-gallon tank. Not far from the Aquarium is the Adler Planetarium where a multimedia sky show is projected on the inside of the domed roof.

Chicago is a city of the arts – of all kinds. Some six hundred newspapers and magazines are published here including the oldest, the *Chicago Tribune,* established in 1847 and helped along its way by Medill,

*Above right* Joan Miró called his sculpture "Chicago" without much imagination, but no one can really tell why. It was a 1981 addition to the Civic Center scene by the Spanish artist and has raised the same kind of speculation as the work by Picasso.

*Below right* Some call it "the Steel Mosquito" though artist Calder gave it the title of "Flamingo". Well, it is red and it does stand three stories high in steel. The delicacy of this enormous metal sculpture can be admired at Chicago's Federal Center Plaza.

*Left* Chicagoans have been asking for years what exactly Picasso's giant sculpture on Daley Plaza is supposed to represent. A primitive African mask? A woman? Or is it an afghan hound? Picasso died in 1973 without giving any answers. As it was a gift to the city, Chicagoans don't complain.

*Below* Several years of effort led to the dedication of Picasso's 50 ft high sculpture now standing at Daley Plaza. The city elders were not exactly taken with its beauty but it seems the children do find a use for it.

Patterson and McCormick. The Hefner Playboy empire also started right here in Chicago, but more significantly there's a large black magazine empire, Johnson Publishing Company, which produces *Ebony*, among others. John H. Johnson founded his company in 1942 with a borrowed $500. Now he not only publishes several periodicals but owns a book division, a radio station and a cosmetics subsidiary.

The early part of the twentieth century saw a splendid renaissance of novels and poetry. It was at this time that Harriet

*Facing page, top* A different kind of artwork stands in Lincoln Park, Chicago's largest recreational area – a north-west Indian totem pole. Many people flock to the green oasis of this park to bike, jog, play ball or visit any of its several attractions.

*Facing page, middle* One of the world's great art museums, the Art Institute of Chicago houses an overwhelming collection of works spanning 40 centuries from antiquities to Impressionists. Look especially for the Thorne Rooms and the transplanted Chicago Stock Exchange Room.

*Facing page, bottom* Adler Planetarium is an attraction in itself, crowned as it is with a lead-covered copper dome and made of rainbow-colored granite. The signs of the Zodiac are featured on bronze plaques at each of the building's 12 outside corners. Inside highlight is the Sky Show.

*Left* The Museum of Science and Industry is one of the best, especially for young people. Exhibits include a fairy-tale castle doll house; a clever circus exhibit and a working coal mine. A display of America's early railroads and a captured German submarine are among other displays.

*Below* The Field Museum houses endless fascinating exhibits on anthropology, ecology, geology. A world famous natural history museum, its dinosaur collection is always among the favorites. Also the pair of fighting elephants located in the main hall.

Monroe founded her magazine *Poetry*, which has since published almost every important poet. The city's most distinguished poet is undoubtedly Carl Sandburg who gave his hometown many of its titles: "city of the big shoulders", "hot butcher to the world", "stacker of wheat".

Another writer, Nelson Algren, shows he knows the city's heart when he writes, "It's every man for himself in this hired air" (*Chicago: City on the Make*), but also adds, "Before you earn the right to rap any sort of joint, you have to love it a little while."

Artworks take all forms in Chicago, more recently as extremely avant garde open-air decoratives. The boom began with Picasso's gift, abstract enough to cause more than a few raised eyebrows. Was this mask-like creation supposed to be a cross-eyed baboon, the face of a woman, or what? Whatever, Chicago has the distinction of having the only civic monument in North America by the world's most famous artist.

Calder's three-story bright red steel work is just as abstract and some have nicknamed it "the steel mosquito". There was amusement in many quarters when Claes Oldenburg was chosen to create a sculpture for the Social Security Building. He came up with "Batcolumn", which stands 100 feet high and comprises 1608 pieces. Then there's a typical Henry Moore entitled "Nuclear Energy" resting appropriately on the site of the first nuclear chain reaction on the University of Chicago campus.

Unusual art is usual in Chicago, witness local sculptor Jerry Peart's "Miss Plutonium" at the Time-Life Building, a colorful if confusing masterpiece, while nobody really knows what Spanish artist Joan Miró's piece represents even if it is called "Chicago". Harry Bertoia's "Sounding Sculpture" at least has a musical sound (created when its metal rods are swayed by the wind).

Art on the inside is just as abundant, only this time you can buy it. A large number of galleries can be found downtown along North Michigan Avenue and its cross-streets like Ontario, but small galleries are scattered throughout the city, and they welcome browsers as much as serious collectors. One of the largest is on the Magnificent Mile – Atlas Galleries, which boasts a first-class selection of limited edition graphics and original oils. Jacques Baruch Gallery has become internationally recognized for its Eastern European prints, and Circle Galleries in the Marriott Hotel is one of the city's most distinguished for fine art graphics.

As for the theater – the major theaters are downtown and include the Blackstone, Goodman, Shubert and Studebaker.

*Right* The Chicago Symphony Orchestra is the third oldest in America and is world renowned. Founded in 1891 it gives performances in Orchestra Hall and other city locations. It is especially praised for its solidarity of tone and excellent brass sections.

*Below* This audience is enjoying one of the city's many musical events.

*Far right, above* "Cinderella" is among the ballets performed annually by the Chicago City Ballet. There is a spring and a fall season at the Auditorium Theater. Classical and modern ballet is also staged in an open air pavilion during the summer Ravinia Festival taking place 25 miles north.

*Far right, below* Chicago is particularly famous for traditional jazz though many of the best joints are located in the black part of town. "Teresa's", pictured here, is one of the oldest and greatest to listen to jazz and blues.

*Right* The arts have always flourished in Chicago, a city which loves opera, ballet and theater. The Chicago Theater pictured here on North State Street Mall is a venue for many types of stage productions. You'll find it in "the Loop" area of town.

*Below* The Lyric Opera House is a home for Chicago's famous opera company seen performing here. Other theaters give half-price day of performance tickets from the Hot Tix booths on South State Street Mall or Oak Park Mall. The city also has a hot line for current entertainment happenings.

# Natural Assets

Chicago began as the crossroads of lake and river traffic. Where the two met there was an Indian settlement surrounded by nothing but prairie. Today there are high-rise towers. Swampland has been filled in as the city expanded, but Chicago's natural assets still remain.

Lake Michigan is the most dominant natural feature. From the air one could be forgiven for thinking that this was the sea. Many handsome buildings are built at lakeshore; many city parks border it. Chicagoans bike alongside it, jog by it, boat on it, swim in it. Status is judged by how far you live from it. There is a beach and eight harbors.

It was Daniel Burnham who laid out a plan for the city's parks, well over five hundred of them stretching for acre after acre. The 17 miles of public beach are clean and the 35 000-plus acres of forest on the outskirts of town provide a rural contrast to the jazzy city.

Lincoln Park was named for President Lincoln and is Chicago's largest park, covering about 1000 acres off the lake from North Avenue to Hollywood. It's a wealthy area best known for its zoo and conservatory. The zoo is home to over 2000 animals and birds, a better-than-ever habitat since its reconstruction was completed in 1982. Favorite areas are the children's zoo and zoo nursery where zoo babies can be seen and petted. The Great Ape House and Sea Lion Pool are equally popular, while at the Bird House a variety of birds have the illusion of freedom in a tropical "free-flight" setting.

Changing floral exhibits bring the seasonal and the exotic to Chicago at the Lincoln Park Conservatory. The Palm House, the Fernery, the Tropical House and the Show House are all filled with colorful blooms, plants and trees, and three outdoor gardens surround them: the Main Garden, Grandmother's Garden, and the Rock Garden planted with native shrubs and wildflowers.

It's easy enough to find a local neighborhood swing. For the more sophisticated kind of joy and thrill rides, head out of town for Marriott's Great America, a theme park full of fun things to see and do. Musical shows are also given here during the summer season.

Grant Park is where those 1968 riots took place during the National Democratic Convention, but it is also where the Grant Park Symphony Orchestra performs in summer and where the annual Jazz Festival is held. This takes place usually in the first week in September – the best jazz, and it's all free.

One of the finest garden attractions is Garfield Park Conservatory, four and a half acres under one glass roof. Some 185 species of tropical plants and trees fill the Palm House and all types of graceful ferns grow in the Fernery. Special floral shows featuring for example the spring azalea and camelia or the Christmas poinsettia are held in the Horticultural Hall. Other attractive and unusual plants are found in the Arid and the Cactus Houses.

Such outdoor areas all lend themselves to sporting activities. The lakeside bike path runs for 11 miles and in summer a Lincoln Park concession rents out bikes. Some of the city's golf courses are along the lakeshore – the best municipal course is in Lincoln Park. So are the best municipal tennis courts. The best city swimming pools are at Wells Park and Gill Park.

Lake swimming is most popular from the beaches to the north of The Loop off Lake

*Above* The shores of Lake Michigan are lined with clean safe beaches. The most fashionable is Oak Street Beach on what Chicagoans call "the Gold Coast", but it does get crowded. Go further north to find fewer people.

*Right* The lakefront is the city's front yard and biking along it is one of the most popular sports. You can bike in either direction from Oak Street Beach known as the "beautiful people beach". The lakeside bike paths run for about 11 miles.

*Left* Lake Michigan is certainly a magnificent natural asset to the city and allows for all types of watersports when the weather's good. Wind surfing is one of them. The wind, by the way, can whip up the lake fiercely and unexpectedly.

*Below* Taking a beach break isn't a bad idea when the cycling gets too tiring. There are 17 miles of public beach and those tired of the sand can enjoy biking through the city parks or the forested preserve on the outskirts of town.

*Far left* These days this square-rigged, three-masted sailing ship is chartered for sightseeing tours. Several companies feature boating trips on lake and river both during the day and for early evening cruises.

*Left* The Chicago Yacht Club on Lake Michigan is one of several marinas. The lake offers superb sailing but is deceptive as any experienced sailor will be quick to explain. Storms of up to 40 knots can blow up quite suddenly so check forecasts first.

*Below* There are some eight harbors along the lake shore where boats may be rented or anchored. In some places sailing instruction is offered; at others, sightseeing boats leave for tours of Chicago's waterways.

Shore Drive, with Oak Street Beach on what is dubbed "The Gold Coast" being the most fashionable. For sailing, one of the most frequented marinas is at Highland Park. Chicago's Forest Preserve is the place for hiking and riding over 200 miles of trails, or biking along its 50 miles of special bike trails. The locals enjoy this area as much in winter when they come to snowmobile or cross-country ski.

The annual entertainment extravaganza is probably "Chicagofest", a celebration that takes place each year in Soldier Field, usually around mid-August. There are numerous venues within Soldier Field; the main stage there accommodates 27 000.

Visitors have a choice of ways to enjoy Chicago's natural beauty spots. Wendella Sightseeing Tours explore the lake and river on 1½ and 2½ hour tours. They are not the only sightseeing boats — others feature daily and nightly excursions on the lake and river. Walking tours are an alternative, either of the Frank Lloyd Wright homes, or the ethnic neighborhoods or the famous buildings.

Not only are the well-known points of interest highlighted, but the lesser ones as well. Many of the not-so-well-known places are featured on tours for the discriminating: an introduction to the city's architecture, the major buildings, the quarters of town, the skyscrapers, the money meccas.

On the outskirts of the city are recreational areas too. The Brookfield Zoo, two hundred acres where the barriers look like natural landscape, is one of the world's

*Above right* Winter at lakefront can mean a thick dusting of snow.

*Below right* A city of commerce it may be but this Midwest city has plenty of greenery, as can be seen from this summer skyline view.

*Below* It may look like the Gulf of Finland but this is the Lincoln Park lagoon, frozen over in winter and most suitable for ice fishing. Chicago's winter months warrant wearing warm clothes — temperatures dip well below zero.

most modern zoos. The wolves have their special woods and so do the bison; and there is a Saharan environment for desert beasts. Marriott's Great America takes care of the under-16s with a variety of themed rides and attractions plus musical shows. Oak Park is a suburb which shows off Frank Lloyd Wright's architecture. There are some 25 buildings from the simple to the gingerbread turreted kind. Walking tours are encouraged here and in spring some of the private homes are open to the public.

It is Chicago's nearby natural assets that have given it its quieter tones. South of the metropolis spread the rich farmlands of Illinois, the land that has made the city rich, the land which gave Lincoln to the nation (he spent much of his adult life in this state). He was the sixteenth President and between 1837 and 1861 he not only practiced law in the state of Illinois but married and raised his family here too. Near the state capital are many historic sites connected with Lincoln.

Chicago is a city with an excellent geographical location; a city blessed by trade. And well equipped with facilities to beat the winter cold.

Sightseeing tours can be either by coach or boat. From May through September, tourist boats cruise Chicago's canal system, river and lake. No hills or mountains, just incredible riches. The site the Indians chose that promised subsequent settlers so much has kept most of its promises. The great Mississippi still flows not far away. Trade excelled because the city reaches to the Atlantic through the Great Lakes and the St Lawrence River. And within five hundred miles are all the coal, iron, oil, black topsoil and hydro-electric power that have made Chicago the Midwest metropolis it is.

*Above right* Sports fans have a choice of stadiums where they can watch their favorite team play their favorite sport. Those who prefer participation to watching use the parks like these rugby players in Lincoln Park.

*Below right* Chicago's North Suburban Forest Preserve and Park is one of the best places for horseback riding and hiking. There are over 200 miles of trails here and 50 miles of special bike trails

*Left* The Chicago Cubs play at Wrigley Field where clever footwork of Tinkers, Evers and Chance inspired a poem, and where Babe Ruth's called-shot home run wrote another of his legendary chapters.

*Below* Wrigley Field is an attraction in itself – it's seen a lot of baseball history. The greats and the not-so-great have done their best or worst for the bleachers audience. Tickets are available at the stadium or any Ticketron outlet.

*Right* It takes "human energy" as this runner proclaims on his T-shirt to run in the Chicago Marathon. For those who seek the exercize without the competition, there's a special jogging path in Lincoln Park.

*Above left* Taking their exercizing seriously, this group enjoys the open air and lakefront for their class. Many top city hotels however offer more private health facilities.

*Below left* Buckingham Fountain in Grant Park holds some 1.5 million gallons of water and the main spout shoots 145 feet into the air. Every evening in season it is illuminated by colorful lights. The fountain was a gift from eccentric and wealthy Kate Buckingham.

*Below* It's the Ribfest in Chicago that brings the people to the park, for one of the great outdoor eating celebrations. It's a huge barbecue competition. Another similar eat-out is when the major restaurants take along their chefs to cook barbecue style.

# Major Attractions

**1 Adler Planetarium** S Lake Shore Dr —.Multimedia sky shows explore the universe and genuine moonrock is on display in the Doane Observatory.

**2 Art Institute of Chicago** Michigan & Adams — Famous for French Impressionist paintings, oriental works, prints and drawings.

**3 Bertoia's Sounding Sculpture** Standard Oil Bldg Plaza, 200 E Randolph — A sculpture with a difference — movement and sound — making music in the wind.

**4 Buckingham Fountain** Lakefront in Grant Park — Double the size of its Versailles prototype, this magnificent fountain is transformed by a colorful light show at night.

**5 Chagall's "The Four Seasons"** Monroe & Dearborn Sts — Marc Chagall's 70 ft long, four-sided mosaic, with outdoor café and summer music events.

**6 Chicago Temple** 77 W Washington St — The world's tallest church, 568 ft high, this Methodist house of worship offers tours of the building including "The Sky Chapel Pilgrimage".

**7 Chinatown** Cermak Rd & Wentworth Ave — A place to enjoy authentic Chinese cuisine in the heart of the city's Chinese-American community.

**8 Field Museum of Natural History** Roosevelt Rd & Lakeshore Dr — Exhibits ranging from prehistoric to space age housed in the Museum's 10 acres of land.

**9 John Hancock Center** 875 N Michigan — From the observation deck of this towering skyscraper you can see Illinois, Indiana, Michigan and Wisconsin.

**10 Lincoln Park Zoo** 2045 N Lincoln Park West — Tigers, lions, apes and sea lions can all be found here in the heart of the city's largest park, and also a Children's Zoo and unusual Farm-in-the-Zoo for younger visitors.

**11 Magnificent Mile** Oak St South to the Chicago River — A mile of exclusive shops ranging from individual boutiques to the famed Water Tower.

**12 Marina City** 300 N State — Two 60-story cylindrical buildings designed to provide a completely self-sufficient living and working environment.

**13 Monadnock Building** 53 W Jackson — In 1893 this was the world's largest office building and is still the highest commercial building with masonry walls.

**14 Museum of Surgical Sciences and Hall of Fame** 1524 N Lake Shore Dr — A museum devoted to the history of medicine and its practitioners, with particular bias towards the development of surgical techniques.

**15 Navy Pier** Grand & Lakefront — The North Promenade offers a spectacular view of the Chicago skyline while from the south side of the pier you can board USS *Silversides,* America's most famous surviving submarine from World War Two.

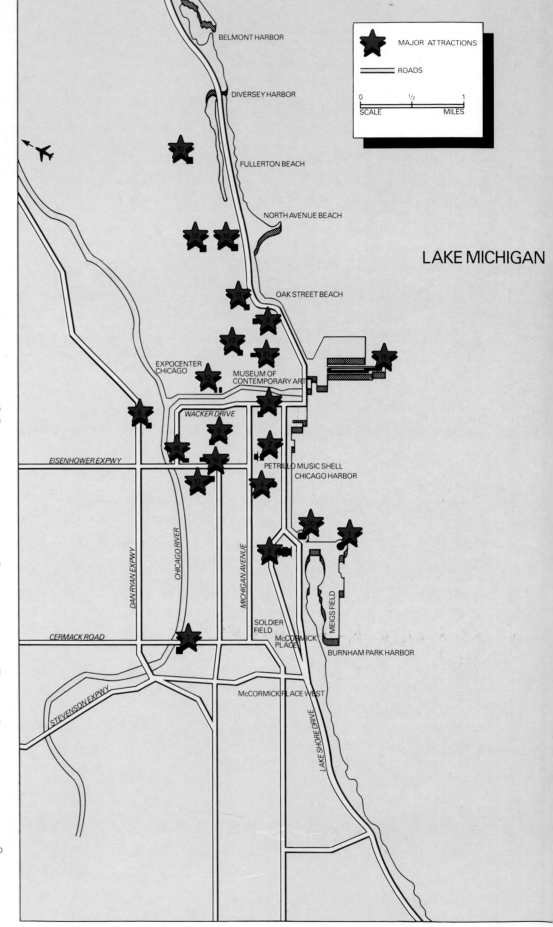

**16 The Rookery** 209 S LaSalle – Designed by Burnham and Root and built in 1886, this is the oldest steel skeleton skyscraper in existence.

**17 Rush Street** Chicago Ave N to Division – The hub of the city's night life entertainment with nightclubs, restaurants, and some venues for jazz and blues.

**18 Sears Tower** Wacker Dr & Jackson – The world's tallest building, 1454 ft high and 110 stories, this provides an enclosed observation deck for wary sightseers.

**19 Ripley's Believe It or Not Museum** 1500 N Wells – World-famous home of strange and bizarre exhibits.

**20 John G Shedd Aquarium** 1200 S Lake Shore Dr – The world's largest indoor aquarium with daily fish feedings in the Coral Reef Tank open to the public.

**21 Water Tower Place** 835 N Michigan – An enormous shopping mall with restaurants and theatres as well as shops, and an impressive seven story atrium.

# PICTURE CREDITS